Tour Memories

Date: _____ to _____

WWW.WILDFLOWERHIPPIE.COM

© 2022 JENNIFER KERR

ALL RIGHTS RESERVED. NO PART OF THIS BOOK MAY BE REPRODUCED OR USED IN ANY MANNER WITHOUT THE PRIOR WRITTEN PERMISSION OF THE COPYRIGHT OWNER.

PAPERBACK: ISBN 978-0-578-28768-3

FIRST PAPERBACK EDITION 2022

BAND:
DATE: VENUE:
SETLIST

HIGHLIGHTS:

AFTERTHOUGHTS:

FACE MELT SCORE: _____   COUCH OR VENUE: _____

FEEL OF THE SHOW

WEATHER

BEST SONG

FAVORITE TRIPPY MOMENT

FAVORITE CROWD MOMENT

FAVORITE BAND MOMENT

MIRACLES THIS SHOW?

VIBE DURING THE SHOW

VIBE AFTER THE SHOW

SOUVENIRS

SNACKS AND THINGS

AFTER SHOW ADVENTURES

SHOW NOTES

BAND:
DATE: **VENUE:**
SETLIST

HIGHLIGHTS:

AFTERTHOUGHTS:

FACE MELT SCORE: _____   COUCH OR VENUE: _____

FEEL OF THE SHOW

WEATHER

BEST SONG

FAVORITE TRIPPY MOMENT

FAVORITE CROWD MOMENT

FAVORITE BAND MOMENT

MIRACLES THIS SHOW?

VIBE DURING THE SHOW

VIBE AFTER THE SHOW

SOUVENIRS

SNACKS AND THINGS

AFTER SHOW ADVENTURES

SHOW NOTES

BAND:
DATE: VENUE:
SETLIST

HIGHLIGHTS:

AFTERTHOUGHTS:

FACE MELT SCORE: _____   COUCH OR VENUE: _____

FEEL OF THE SHOW

WEATHER

BEST SONG

FAVORITE TRIPPY MOMENT

FAVORITE CROWD MOMENT

FAVORITE BAND MOMENT

MIRACLES THIS SHOW?

VIBE DURING THE SHOW

VIBE AFTER THE SHOW

SOUVENIRS

SNACKS AND THINGS

AFTER SHOW ADVENTURES

SHOW NOTES

BAND:
DATE: VENUE:
SETLIST

HIGHLIGHTS:

AFTERTHOUGHTS:

FACE MELT SCORE: _____   COUCH OR VENUE: _____

FEEL OF THE SHOW

WEATHER

BEST SONG

FAVORITE TRIPPY MOMENT

FAVORITE CROWD MOMENT

FAVORITE BAND MOMENT

MIRACLES THIS SHOW?

VIBE DURING THE SHOW

VIBE AFTER THE SHOW

SOUVENIRS

SNACKS AND THINGS

AFTER SHOW ADVENTURES

SHOW NOTES

SLAP YOUR TICKET STUB, MEMORABILIA AND DOODLES HERE

BAND:

DATE: **VENUE:**

SETLIST

HIGHLIGHTS:

AFTERTHOUGHTS:

FACE MELT SCORE: _____   COUCH OR VENUE: _____

FEEL OF THE SHOW

WEATHER

BEST SONG

FAVORITE TRIPPY MOMENT

FAVORITE CROWD MOMENT

FAVORITE BAND MOMENT

MIRACLES THIS SHOW?

VIBE DURING THE SHOW

VIBE AFTER THE SHOW

SOUVENIRS

SNACKS AND THINGS

AFTER SHOW ADVENTURES

SHOW NOTES

BAND:
DATE: VENUE:
SETLIST

HIGHLIGHTS:

AFTERTHOUGHTS:

FACE MELT SCORE: _____   COUCH OR VENUE: _____

FEEL OF THE SHOW

WEATHER

BEST SONG

FAVORITE TRIPPY MOMENT

FAVORITE CROWD MOMENT

FAVORITE BAND MOMENT

MIRACLES THIS SHOW?

VIBE DURING THE SHOW

VIBE AFTER THE SHOW

SOUVENIRS

SNACKS AND THINGS

AFTER SHOW ADVENTURES

SHOW NOTES

BAND:
DATE: **VENUE:**
SETLIST

HIGHLIGHTS:

AFTERTHOUGHTS:

FACE MELT SCORE: _____   COUCH OR VENUE: _____

FEEL OF THE SHOW

WEATHER

BEST SONG

FAVORITE TRIPPY MOMENT

FAVORITE CROWD MOMENT

FAVORITE BAND MOMENT

MIRACLES THIS SHOW?

VIBE DURING THE SHOW

VIBE AFTER THE SHOW

SOUVENIRS

SNACKS AND THINGS

AFTER SHOW ADVENTURES

SHOW NOTES

BAND:
DATE: VENUE:
SETLIST

HIGHLIGHTS:

AFTERTHOUGHTS:

FACE MELT SCORE: _____   COUCH OR VENUE: _____

FEEL OF THE SHOW

WEATHER

BEST SONG

FAVORITE TRIPPY MOMENT

FAVORITE CROWD MOMENT

FAVORITE BAND MOMENT

MIRACLES THIS SHOW?

VIBE DURING THE SHOW

VIBE AFTER THE SHOW

SOUVENIRS

SNACKS AND THINGS

AFTER SHOW ADVENTURES

SHOW NOTES

BAND:
DATE: VENUE:
SETLIST

HIGHLIGHTS:

AFTERTHOUGHTS:

FACE MELT SCORE: _____   COUCH OR VENUE: _____

FEEL OF THE SHOW

WEATHER

BEST SONG

FAVORITE TRIPPY MOMENT

FAVORITE CROWD MOMENT

FAVORITE BAND MOMENT

MIRACLES THIS SHOW?

VIBE DURING THE SHOW

VIBE AFTER THE SHOW

SOUVENIRS

SNACKS AND THINGS

AFTER SHOW ADVENTURES

SHOW NOTES

SLAP YOUR TICKET STUB, MEMORABILIA AND DOODLES HERE

BAND:
DATE: VENUE:
SETLIST

HIGHLIGHTS:

AFTERTHOUGHTS:

FACE MELT SCORE: _____ COUCH OR VENUE: _____

FEEL OF THE SHOW

WEATHER

BEST SONG

FAVORITE TRIPPY MOMENT

FAVORITE CROWD MOMENT

FAVORITE BAND MOMENT

MIRACLES THIS SHOW?

VIBE DURING THE SHOW

VIBE AFTER THE SHOW

SOUVENIRS

SNACKS AND THINGS

AFTER SHOW ADVENTURES

SHOW NOTES

SLAP YOUR TICKET STUB, MEMORABILIA AND DOODLES HERE

BAND:
DATE: **VENUE:**
SETLIST

HIGHLIGHTS:

AFTERTHOUGHTS:

FACE MELT SCORE: _____   COUCH OR VENUE: _____

FEEL OF THE SHOW

WEATHER

BEST SONG

FAVORITE TRIPPY MOMENT

FAVORITE CROWD MOMENT

FAVORITE BAND MOMENT

MIRACLES THIS SHOW?

VIBE DURING THE SHOW

VIBE AFTER THE SHOW

SOUVENIRS

SNACKS AND THINGS

AFTER SHOW ADVENTURES

SHOW NOTES

SLAP YOUR TICKET STUB, MEMORABILIA AND DOODLES HERE

BAND:
DATE: VENUE:
SETLIST

HIGHLIGHTS:

AFTERTHOUGHTS:

FACE MELT SCORE: _____   COUCH OR VENUE: _____

FEEL OF THE SHOW

WEATHER

BEST SONG

FAVORITE TRIPPY MOMENT

FAVORITE CROWD MOMENT

FAVORITE BAND MOMENT

MIRACLES THIS SHOW?

VIBE DURING THE SHOW

VIBE AFTER THE SHOW

SOUVENIRS

SNACKS AND THINGS

AFTER SHOW ADVENTURES

SHOW NOTES

SLAP YOUR TICKET STUB, MEMORABILIA AND DOODLES HERE

BAND:
DATE: **VENUE:**
SETLIST

HIGHLIGHTS:

AFTERTHOUGHTS:

FACE MELT SCORE: _____   COUCH OR VENUE: _____

FEEL OF THE SHOW

WEATHER

BEST SONG

FAVORITE TRIPPY MOMENT

FAVORITE CROWD MOMENT

FAVORITE BAND MOMENT

MIRACLES THIS SHOW?

VIBE DURING THE SHOW

VIBE AFTER THE SHOW

SOUVENIRS

SNACKS AND THINGS

AFTER SHOW ADVENTURES

SHOW NOTES

SLAP YOUR TICKET STUB, MEMORABILIA AND DOODLES HERE

BAND:
DATE: VENUE:
SETLIST

HIGHLIGHTS:

AFTERTHOUGHTS:

FACE MELT SCORE: _____   COUCH OR VENUE: _____

FEEL OF THE SHOW

WEATHER

BEST SONG

FAVORITE TRIPPY MOMENT

FAVORITE CROWD MOMENT

FAVORITE BAND MOMENT

MIRACLES THIS SHOW?

VIBE DURING THE SHOW

VIBE AFTER THE SHOW

SOUVENIRS

SNACKS AND THINGS

AFTER SHOW ADVENTURES

SHOW NOTES

SLAP YOUR TICKET STUB, MEMORABILIA AND DOODLES HERE

BAND:
DATE: VENUE:
SETLIST

HIGHLIGHTS:

AFTERTHOUGHTS:

FACE MELT SCORE: _____   COUCH OR VENUE: _____

FEEL OF THE SHOW

WEATHER

BEST SONG

FAVORITE TRIPPY MOMENT

FAVORITE CROWD MOMENT

FAVORITE BAND MOMENT

MIRACLES THIS SHOW?

VIBE DURING THE SHOW

VIBE AFTER THE SHOW

SOUVENIRS

SNACKS AND THINGS

AFTER SHOW ADVENTURES

SHOW NOTES

SLAP YOUR TICKET STUB, MEMORABILIA AND DOODLES HERE

BAND:
DATE: VENUE:
SETLIST

HIGHLIGHTS:

AFTERTHOUGHTS:

FACE MELT SCORE: _____   COUCH OR VENUE: _____

FEEL OF THE SHOW

WEATHER

BEST SONG

FAVORITE TRIPPY MOMENT

FAVORITE CROWD MOMENT

FAVORITE BAND MOMENT

MIRACLES THIS SHOW?

VIBE DURING THE SHOW

VIBE AFTER THE SHOW

SOUVENIRS

SNACKS AND THINGS

AFTER SHOW ADVENTURES

SHOW NOTES

SLAP YOUR TICKET STUB, MEMORABILIA AND DOODLES HERE

BAND:
DATE: **VENUE:**

SETLIST

HIGHLIGHTS:

AFTERTHOUGHTS:

FACE MELT SCORE: _____   COUCH OR VENUE: _____

FEEL OF THE SHOW

WEATHER

BEST SONG

FAVORITE TRIPPY MOMENT

FAVORITE CROWD MOMENT

FAVORITE BAND MOMENT

MIRACLES THIS SHOW?

VIBE DURING THE SHOW

VIBE AFTER THE SHOW

SOUVENIRS

SNACKS AND THINGS

AFTER SHOW ADVENTURES

SHOW NOTES

SLAP YOUR TICKET STUB, MEMORABILIA AND DOODLES HERE

BAND:
DATE: VENUE:
SETLIST

HIGHLIGHTS:

AFTERTHOUGHTS:

FACE MELT SCORE: _____   COUCH OR VENUE: _____

FEEL OF THE SHOW

WEATHER

BEST SONG

FAVORITE TRIPPY MOMENT

FAVORITE CROWD MOMENT

FAVORITE BAND MOMENT

MIRACLES THIS SHOW?

VIBE DURING THE SHOW

VIBE AFTER THE SHOW

SOUVENIRS

SNACKS AND THINGS

AFTER SHOW ADVENTURES

SHOW NOTES

SLAP YOUR TICKET STUB, MEMORABILIA AND DOODLES HERE

BAND:

DATE: **VENUE:**

SETLIST

HIGHLIGHTS:

AFTERTHOUGHTS:

FACE MELT SCORE: _____ COUCH OR VENUE: _____

FEEL OF THE SHOW

WEATHER

BEST SONG

FAVORITE TRIPPY MOMENT

FAVORITE CROWD MOMENT

FAVORITE BAND MOMENT

MIRACLES THIS SHOW?

VIBE DURING THE SHOW

VIBE AFTER THE SHOW

SOUVENIRS

SNACKS AND THINGS

AFTER SHOW ADVENTURES

SHOW NOTES

SLAP YOUR TICKET STUB, MEMORABILIA AND DOODLES HERE

BAND:
DATE: VENUE:
SETLIST

HIGHLIGHTS:

AFTERTHOUGHTS:

FACE MELT SCORE: _____   COUCH OR VENUE: _____

FEEL OF THE SHOW

WEATHER

BEST SONG

FAVORITE TRIPPY MOMENT

FAVORITE CROWD MOMENT

FAVORITE BAND MOMENT

MIRACLES THIS SHOW?

VIBE DURING THE SHOW

VIBE AFTER THE SHOW

SOUVENIRS

SNACKS AND THINGS

AFTER SHOW ADVENTURES

SHOW NOTES

SLAP YOUR TICKET STUB, MEMORABILIA AND DOODLES HERE

BAND:
DATE: VENUE:

SETLIST

HIGHLIGHTS:

AFTERTHOUGHTS:

FACE MELT SCORE: _____ COUCH OR VENUE: _____

FEEL OF THE SHOW

WEATHER

BEST SONG

FAVORITE TRIPPY MOMENT

FAVORITE CROWD MOMENT

FAVORITE BAND MOMENT

MIRACLES THIS SHOW?

VIBE DURING THE SHOW

VIBE AFTER THE SHOW

SOUVENIRS

SNACKS AND THINGS

AFTER SHOW ADVENTURES

SHOW NOTES

SLAP YOUR TICKET STUB, MEMORABILIA AND DOODLES HERE

BAND:
DATE: VENUE:
SETLIST

HIGHLIGHTS:

AFTERTHOUGHTS:

FACE MELT SCORE: _____ COUCH OR VENUE: _____

FEEL OF THE SHOW

WEATHER

BEST SONG

FAVORITE TRIPPY MOMENT

FAVORITE CROWD MOMENT

FAVORITE BAND MOMENT

MIRACLES THIS SHOW?

VIBE DURING THE SHOW

VIBE AFTER THE SHOW

SOUVENIRS

SNACKS AND THINGS

AFTER SHOW ADVENTURES

SHOW NOTES

SLAP YOUR TICKET STUB, MEMORABILIA AND DOODLES HERE

BAND:
DATE: VENUE:

SETLIST

HIGHLIGHTS:

AFTERTHOUGHTS:

FACE MELT SCORE: _____   COUCH OR VENUE: _____

FEEL OF THE SHOW

WEATHER

BEST SONG

FAVORITE TRIPPY MOMENT

FAVORITE CROWD MOMENT

FAVORITE BAND MOMENT

MIRACLES THIS SHOW?

VIBE DURING THE SHOW

VIBE AFTER THE SHOW

SOUVENIRS

SNACKS AND THINGS

AFTER SHOW ADVENTURES

SHOW NOTES

SLAP YOUR TICKET STUB, MEMORABILIA AND DOODLES HERE

BAND:

DATE: **VENUE:**

SETLIST

HIGHLIGHTS:

AFTERTHOUGHTS:

FACE MELT SCORE: _____   COUCH OR VENUE: _____

FEEL OF THE SHOW

WEATHER

BEST SONG

FAVORITE TRIPPY MOMENT

FAVORITE CROWD MOMENT

FAVORITE BAND MOMENT

MIRACLES THIS SHOW?

VIBE DURING THE SHOW

VIBE AFTER THE SHOW

SOUVENIRS

SNACKS AND THINGS

AFTER SHOW ADVENTURES

SHOW NOTES

SLAP YOUR TICKET STUB, MEMORABILIA AND DOODLES HERE

BAND:
DATE: VENUE:
SETLIST

HIGHLIGHTS:

AFTERTHOUGHTS:

FACE MELT SCORE: _____   COUCH OR VENUE: _____

FEEL OF THE SHOW

WEATHER

BEST SONG

FAVORITE TRIPPY MOMENT

FAVORITE CROWD MOMENT

FAVORITE BAND MOMENT

MIRACLES THIS SHOW?

VIBE DURING THE SHOW

VIBE AFTER THE SHOW

SOUVENIRS

SNACKS AND THINGS

AFTER SHOW ADVENTURES

SHOW NOTES

SLAP YOUR TICKET STUB, MEMORABILIA AND DOODLES HERE

BAND:
DATE: VENUE:
SETLIST

HIGHLIGHTS:

AFTERTHOUGHTS:

FACE MELT SCORE: _____ COUCH OR VENUE: _____

FEEL OF THE SHOW

WEATHER

BEST SONG

FAVORITE TRIPPY MOMENT

FAVORITE CROWD MOMENT

FAVORITE BAND MOMENT

MIRACLES THIS SHOW?

VIBE DURING THE SHOW

VIBE AFTER THE SHOW

SOUVENIRS

SNACKS AND THINGS

AFTER SHOW ADVENTURES

SHOW NOTES

SLAP YOUR TICKET STUB, MEMORABILIA AND DOODLES HERE

BAND:
DATE: VENUE:
SETLIST

HIGHLIGHTS:

AFTERTHOUGHTS:

FACE MELT SCORE: _____   COUCH OR VENUE: _____

FEEL OF THE SHOW

WEATHER

BEST SONG

FAVORITE TRIPPY MOMENT

FAVORITE CROWD MOMENT

FAVORITE BAND MOMENT

MIRACLES THIS SHOW?

VIBE DURING THE SHOW

VIBE AFTER THE SHOW

SOUVENIRS

SNACKS AND THINGS

AFTER SHOW ADVENTURES

SHOW NOTES

SLAP YOUR TICKET STUB, MEMORABILIA AND DOODLES HERE

BAND:
DATE: **VENUE:**
SETLIST

HIGHLIGHTS:

AFTERTHOUGHTS:

FACE MELT SCORE: _____   COUCH OR VENUE: _____

FEEL OF THE SHOW

WEATHER

BEST SONG

FAVORITE TRIPPY MOMENT

FAVORITE CROWD MOMENT

FAVORITE BAND MOMENT

MIRACLES THIS SHOW?

VIBE DURING THE SHOW

VIBE AFTER THE SHOW

SOUVENIRS

SNACKS AND THINGS

AFTER SHOW ADVENTURES

SHOW NOTES

SLAP YOUR TICKET STUB, MEMORABILIA AND DOODLES HERE

BAND:
DATE: VENUE:

SETLIST

HIGHLIGHTS:

AFTERTHOUGHTS:

FACE MELT SCORE: _____ COUCH OR VENUE: _____

FEEL OF THE SHOW

WEATHER

BEST SONG

FAVORITE TRIPPY MOMENT

FAVORITE CROWD MOMENT

FAVORITE BAND MOMENT

MIRACLES THIS SHOW?

VIBE DURING THE SHOW

VIBE AFTER THE SHOW

SOUVENIRS

SNACKS AND THINGS

AFTER SHOW ADVENTURES

SHOW NOTES

SLAP YOUR TICKET STUB, MEMORABILIA AND DOODLES HERE

BAND:
DATE: VENUE:
SETLIST

HIGHLIGHTS:

AFTERTHOUGHTS:

FACE MELT SCORE: _____   COUCH OR VENUE: _____

FEEL OF THE SHOW

WEATHER

BEST SONG

FAVORITE TRIPPY MOMENT

FAVORITE CROWD MOMENT

FAVORITE BAND MOMENT

MIRACLES THIS SHOW?

VIBE DURING THE SHOW

VIBE AFTER THE SHOW

SOUVENIRS

SNACKS AND THINGS

AFTER SHOW ADVENTURES

SHOW NOTES

SLAP YOUR TICKET STUB, MEMORABILIA AND DOODLES HERE

Other Stuff

CPSIA information can be obtained
at www.ICGtesting.com
Printed in the USA
BVHW040225141222
654203BV00005B/216

9 780578 287683